A Year with John Wesley
and
Our Methodist Values

A Year with John Wesley
and
Our Methodist Values

Michael J. Coyner ■ *Henry H. Knight III*
Sarah Heaner Lancaster ■ *Randy L. Maddox*
F. Douglas Powe Jr.

DISCIPLESHIP RESOURCES

PO BOX 340003 • NASHVILLE, TN 37203-0003
www.discipleshipresources.org

Cover design by Studiohaus
Interior design by PerfectType

Library of Congress Control Number: 2008922165
ISBN 13: 978-0-88177-550-1

CONTENTS

December

INTRODUCTION

THE UNITED METHODIST COUNCIL of Bishops calls the Church to intensive study of and reflection on our Wesleyan theology, polity, and practice. The Council of Bishops believes that the Church needs to teach and we need to learn much about the historical, theological, and biblical roots of our religious traditions, often described as "the United Methodist Way." While many people in our churches, both clergy and laity alike, know basic facts and information about Wesleyan theology and practice, there is not great depth of knowledge found across our Church. Thus, our Bishops seek to engage the Church's interest in and commitment to learning deeply about our heritage in order to influence our patterns and practices of ministry in the future.

Randy Maddox, one of the contributors to this resource, challenges United Methodists to get "the United Methodist Way" into our very bones. Do we act, live, and breathe our faith? Do we know what we believe? Can the people in our churches describe who we are as United Methodists, and can they have conversation with others about our traditions, patterns, and practices of ministry? Do those who watch us as United Methodists see a different kind of people because of the ways we live out our faith in the Church and in the world?

Recently, I had the experience of traveling on a hotel van. As we drove along, conversation naturally ensued. The van driver asked, "Are you a Methodist?" My surprised answer was, "Yes. How did you know that?" He replied, "I don't know. There's just something about the way you talk to me that makes me think that you are a Methodist." Months later, I am still puzzling over this conversation. What did this van driver see? What did I do and/or say? How did I communicate my theological and faith tradition to him?

I believe that the bishops of our Church seek to harness the knowledge and traditions of our Wesleyan and United Methodist heritage in order to move the Church toward new ways of considering how we will live faithfully in the future as disciples of Jesus Christ. In order to assist this effort, the General Board of Discipleship has worked with Bishop Michael Coyner and Dr. Randy Maddox to recruit a number of Wesleyan scholars for this resource, *A Year with John Wesley and Our Methodist Values*. These scholars have contributed twelve reflections on various areas of Wesleyan theology, polity, and practice. Bishop Coyner has developed monthly practices that correspond to each of the twelve reflections. Through monthly attention to these reflections and practices, the Bishops and these Wesleyan scholars hope that new engagement with "the United Methodist Way" will occur across our Church. As an extension of in-depth learning, we believe that more and more people will say to us, "Are you a United Methodist?" We may then engage them in conversation about our faith and our Church so that more and more people choose to live as committed and faithful disciples of Jesus Christ who live as God's transforming agents throughout the world.

Rev. Karen A. Greenwaldt
General Secretary
General Board of Discipleship
The United Methodist Church

JANUARY

John Wesley on the Dedicated Christian Life

Randy L. Maddox

ONE OF THE CENTRAL THEMES running through the breadth of John Wesley's writings is the importance of dedicating oneself—heart and life—to God, following the model of Jesus Christ.

Wesley imbibed this emphasis from his parents. His studies reinforced it. As recorded in the opening of *A Plain Account of Christian Perfection*, Wesley read Jeremy Taylor's *Rule and Exercises of Holy Living and Dying* when he was twenty-three, which led him to "dedicate *all my life* to God; *all* my thoughts, and words, and actions." Shortly after, he read Thomas à Kempis's *Imitation of Christ*, which helped him to see that giving "*all my life* to God (supposing it possible to do this and go no farther) would profit me nothing, unless I gave *my heart*." This classic text by Kempis had such an impact on Wesley that in 1735 he issued an abridgement titled *The Christian's Pattern* as one of his first publications.

Occasionally, "works righteousness" characterizes this emphasis of the early Wesley, with the implication that he set it aside when he came to appreciate God's "free grace" in 1738. However, this is a misunderstanding of the freedom grace brings. For Wesley, the grace of God is not only the unmerited mercy by which we are *free from* the guilt of our sin, but it is also the power of the Holy Spirit poured into our lives, setting us *free for* renewed obedience to God. If there is anything distinct in Wesley's preaching about the importance of submitting to God's ways after 1738, it is the stronger emphasis that "every command in holy writ is only a covered promise," as he put it in his fifth discourse on the Sermon on the Mount (par. II.3). Wesley reminds his hearers in this sermon of God's promise in Jeremiah 31:31 to write the covenant on our hearts. The God of grace does not set aside the law; rather God graciously enables our fulfillment of it.

While God's grace is freeing, it is also resistible. Wesley stressed this balance in his classic sermon "On Working Out Our Own Salvation," affirming that it is only because of the power of the Holy Spirit that we *can* work out our salvation, but adding that we *must* join as "workers together with God" in this journey. In other sermons, Wesley makes clear that God graciously invites us to be fellow workers not only in our own salvation, but also in God's larger redeeming work in the world. As a means of encouraging his people to embrace this call, dedicating the whole of their lives to God, Wesley printed an extract of *The Christian Pattern* repeatedly throughout his ministry.

The mature Wesley also came to appreciate that the interactive nature of God's empowerment and our response meant that the dedication of oneself to God, like every other dimension of the *way* of salvation, was open to breach as well as to deepened commitment. This awareness led him in 1755 to introduce in the Methodist societies a practice of regular *renewal* of one's dedication to God, adapting Richard Alleine's covenant renewal service. This service soon became a yearly staple of Methodist life and has proven for many an effective means of deepening dedication to God.

January: A Time to Renew Our Covenant with God

Bishop Coyner

THERE IS NOTHING MAGICAL about the flip of the calendar from the old year to the New Year, even though eighty-eight percent of all Americans make New Year's resolutions each year. In the United States before 9/11, the number-one resolution was to "lose weight." After 9/11 that changed to "spend more time with my family." Somehow, even American culture senses a need for a change, a fresh start, and a new beginning.

As United Methodists, the month of January offers us the opportunity to make that new beginning in the Wesleyan tradition by reaffirming our covenant with God. Scripture teaches us that God's covenant with us is eternal and calls us to recommit our lives to God. In Jesus Christ, we see the fulfillment of the promise in Jeremiah 31:31-34 of a new covenant, written upon our hearts.

Wesley wrote a Covenant Prayer that can be used in a variety of worship and educational settings. It is number 607 in *The United Methodist Hymnal*:

I am no longer my own, but thine.
Put me to what thou wilt, rank me with whom thou wilt.
Put me to doing, put me to suffering.
Let me be employed by thee or laid aside for thee,
    exalted for thee or brought low by thee.
Let me be full, let me be empty.
Let me have all things, let me have nothing.
I freely and heartily yield all things
    to thy pleasure and disposal.
And now, O glorious and blessed God,

Father, Son, and Holy Spirit,
    thou art mine, and I am thine. So be it.
And the covenant which I have made on earth,
    let it be ratified in heaven. Amen.

January is also a good time to invite people to join a Covenant Disciple Group, and many congregations offer training for new officers and leaders who begin serving in the New Year. Some congregations offer a New Year's Eve Watch Night Service as a way of helping people to reaffirm their covenant with God. One helpful model is the "Covenant Renewal Service" (*The United Methodist Book of Worship*, page 288), but it is possible to use elements of this service on Sunday mornings in January, too. Dan Benedict reminds us of our need for such a time of covenant renewal:

At the heart of Christian devotion is a sense that we are not our own, but that through God's claim upon us in Christ through baptism, we are God's servants. From time to time, Christians need to make a solemn renewal of the covenant, lest we hold back from God what we once gave to God but over time have hoarded for ourselves.

Let January be a time for renewing your covenant with God, both individually and as a congregation.

Hymn by Charles Wesley

Come, Let Us Use the Grace Divine

Come, let us use the grace divine, and all with one accord,
    In a perpetual covenant join ourselves to Christ the Lord;
Give up ourselves, thru Jesus' power, his name to glorify;
    And promise, in this sacred hour, for God to live and die.

The covenant we this moment make be ever kept in mind;
    We will no more our God forsake, or cast these words behind.
We never will throw off the fear of God who hears our vow;
    And if thou art well pleased to hear, come down and meet us now.

Thee, Father, Son, and Holy Ghost, let all our hearts receive,
    Present with thy celestial host the peaceful answer give;
To each covenant the blood apply which takes our sins away,
    And register our names on high and keep us to that day!

The United Methodist Hymnal, #606

FEBRUARY

John Wesley on Justifying Grace and New Life in Christ

Henry H. Knight III

SUPPOSE YOU HAD A TERMINAL ILLNESS but did not know it. You would think everything is normal because everything *seems* normal, until at some point you looked at your life from an entirely different angle. Then, what omce seemed so natural would be seen for what it really is: symptoms of a sickness unto death.

Perhaps, if you found yourself in this condition, you could mitigate the symptoms and try to live as healthy a life as possible under the circumstances. But you cannot cure the disease. To do that, you need outside help—you need a physician.

This is our spiritual condition as seen by John Wesley. Sin is not only in our intentions and our in actions; it is a disease that has infected our very being. Though we have been created in the loving image of the Triune God, sin corrupts that image in such a way that it touches every aspect of our lives. When we come to realize that the things which seem so normal in our culture—possessing more than we need while ignoring the needs of others, centering our lives on things rather than on God, choosing self-gratification instead of self-giving—are but symptoms of this fatal disease of sin, we recognize our need for a physician.

Our problem is worse yet, for we are alienated from the very physician who can cure us! We have, after all, ignored many of the warning signs. We have tried to pretend we were all right, even when there were indications to the contrary. Like a person who doesn't want a physical for fear of what he or she may find, we would rather keep the doctor at a distance and pretend all is well.

Fortunately, we have a physician who is not content to see us destroy our lives—and those of our neighbors—in this way. This physician takes the initiative: "God proves his love for us in that while we were still sinners Christ died for us" (Romans 5:8). It is here that the analogy breaks down. At this point, we have to speak of the wonder of a love almost beyond imagining. Charles Wesley put it this way:

> O Love divine: What hast thou done!
> Th' immortal God hath died for me!
> The Father's co-eternal Son
> Bore all my sins upon the tree.
> Th' immortal God for me hath died,
> My Lord, my love is crucified.

The United Methodist Hymnal, #287

We may be sinners standing before a holy God. We may be creatures standing before our Creator. But we are *loved* by God, even unto death on a cross. Our lives have an infinite worth because an Infinite God has loved us so much.

Through the cross, we are justified and forgiven. John Wesley calls justification a *relative* change, a change in our relationship with God. The gap separating us from God has been bridged. We accept this gracious gift through faith, trusting in what God has done for us in Christ for our justification. Our relationship with the physician is restored.

Just as we might walk through the door of a clinic, trusting in the physician, so we walk through the door of justification, trusting in Jesus Christ. It is then that the Holy Spirit can begin to cure the disease of sin. The resulting transformation that turns us in the direction of ever-increasing health is the new birth, the restorative process is sanctification, and the sign of health is a growing love for God and our neighbor. Wesley calls this a *real* change, an inward renewal by the power of God, the beginning of new life.

Hymn by Charles Wesley

And Can It Be that I Should Gain

And can it be that I should gain an interest in the Savior's blood!
  Died he for me? Who caused his pain! For me? Who him to death pursued?
Amazing love! How can it be that thou, my God, shouldst die for me?
  Amazing love! How can it be that thou, my God, shouldst die for me?

Long my imprisoned spirit lay, fast bound in sin and nature's night;
  Thine eye diffused a quickening ray; I woke, the dungeon flamed with light;
My chains fell off, my heart was free, I rose, went forth, and followed thee.
  My chains fell off, my heart was free, I rose, went forth, and followed thee.

The United Methodist Hymnal, #363

February: A Time to Call for Commitment to Christ

Bishop Coyner

THE MONTH OF FEBRUARY often includes Ash Wednesday and the beginning of the season of Lent. It also includes the Valentine's Day celebration in our U.S. culture, which we can affirm as United Methodists, but our Wesleyan tradition challenges us to expand our concept of "true love." As followers of Jesus Christ, the Shema of the Old Testament expresses our true love: "You shall love the Lord Your God with all your heart, mind, soul, and strength" (Deuteronomy 6:4–5). This is the first of the Ten Commandments, and it reminds us that we owe our first love to God.

The Wesleyan revival in England and America was a call to individuals to make their commitment to Christ in what Wesley understood to be the "justifying grace" of God, which restores our relationship with God. Our Wesleyan way of discipleship affirms that God's grace saves us and begins our process toward sanctification or wholeness. Becoming a follower of Christ is not our doing; it is our response to what God has done for us in the sacrifice of Jesus Christ. Many United Methodist congregations begin Lent by placing a large, rough-hewn wooden cross in the sanctuary. Such a stark reminder of the sacrifice of Christ is a call to receive God's justifying grace.

February is a month when United Methodists can offer this new life in Christ to all who stand outside of a relationship with God. For some congregations, this might include an Ash Wednesday worship service that reminds us we are "dust" and we need to "repent and believe the gospel." For other congregations, the month of February can be a time for revival services, for Lay Witness Missions, or for other times of repentance and renewal.

February is a good time to teach the Ten Commandments to our children and youth and to use them in worship services for all ages. Elton Trueblood has written those commands in a helpful, positive style:

Above all else love God alone;
Bow down to neither wood nor stone.
God's name refuse to take in vain;
The Sabbath rest with care maintain.
Respect your parents all your days;

Hold sacred human life always.
Be loyal to your chosen mate;
Steal nothing, neither small nor great.
Report with truth your neighbor's deed;
And rid your mind of selfish greed.[1]

New life in Christ is more than just obeying these commandments, as important as they are. New life in Christ comes as we accept the gift of God's justifying grace through Jesus Christ. February is a time for all United Methodists to affirm that gift and to offer it to everyone.

[1] Elton Trueblood, *Foundations for Reconstruction* (Harper & Brothers, first edition, 1946).

MARCH

John Wesley's Call to Personal and Social Holiness

F. Douglas Powe Jr.

PEOPLE DO NOT OFTEN confront us by asking, "Is the love of God shed abroad in your heart?" John Wesley believed that this was an important question and one that all Methodists (indeed, all Christians) should be able to answer affirmatively. For Wesley, the core of the Christian journey was a heart so filled with love that there was no room for anything else. The theological language we use in Methodism to describe this is "holiness of heart and life."

Wesley understood the journey into holiness to be a movement toward becoming fully human, as Christ was fully human. He described it in the following way:

For what is holiness, according to the oracles of God? Not bare religion, external religion, a round of outward duties, how many soever they be, and how exactly soever performed. No; gospel holiness is no less than the image of God stamped on the heart. It is no other than the whole mind which was in Christ Jesus ("The New Birth," II.5).

This is something far different from the caricatures that equate concern for "holiness" with insistence on a lifestyle or set of practices that emphasize one's superiority to the rest of humanity. It is instead coming to embody the love exemplified by Christ in one's relationships with God and with others. As Wesley understood, such transformation is possible only as we experience the liberating and empowering presence of God's love, shed abroad in our hearts by the Holy Spirit.

Wesley insisted that the holiness that characterizes authentic Christian life is more than just our external relationship to Christ. It is deeply personal in character, a transformation of our very nature. To use Pauline language, it is becoming a new person in Christ. The process of this transformation is also personal. It is not simply infused in us by God, but is nurtured through grace as we participate regularly in the means God has ordained—including, among others, prayer, study of scripture, participation in Holy Communion, and our conversations. This means that holiness is not something we achieve quickly, moving then to the next thing in life.

Neither is true Christian holiness something that we achieve on our own. One of Wesley's strongest emphases was that "there is no holiness, but social holiness."[2] People often take this as a statement about the importance of social service or social transformation. But Wesley's concern in this statement was to highlight the vital role the surrounding community of Christian believers plays in an individual's journey toward holiness. We need the support of a community, serving as agents of the Divine love that empowers our transformation. Just as importantly, we need the voices and ears of other Christians to check our self-deceptions and hold us accountable to our life of discipleship.

Wesley had no doubt that Christians should reach out in love to those who are sick, in prison, or downtrodden. His diagnosis of the reason that so few did engage in such acts of mercy or efforts for social justice was that they were not yet renewed in holiness. What he offered in his day, and would commend to United Methodists today, was a winsome vision of the renewal God is seeking to work in our lives and a balanced emphasis on the personal and social dimensions of the means of grace that nurture this renewal.

Hymn by Charles Wesley
O Come and Dwell in Me

O come and dwell in me, Spirit of power within,
And bring the glorious liberty from sorrow, fear, and sin.

Hasten the joyful day which shall my sins consume,
When old things shall be done away, and all things new become.

I want the witness, Lord, that all I do is right,
According to thy mind and word, well-pleasing in thy sight.

The United Methodist Hymnal, #388

---

[2] John Wesley, preface to *Hymns and Sacred Poems* (1739), ¶5, *Works* (Jackson) 14:321.

March: A Time to Grow in Personal and Social Holiness

Bishop Coyner

THE MONTH OF MARCH includes the "One Great Hour of Sharing" offering in which we United Methodists emphasize giving for the needs of others. This passion for giving is a distinct aspect of our Wesleyan tradition and an important part of our discipleship in the United Methodist Church.

Wesley claimed, "The world is my parish," and as descendants of Wesley we make that claim, too. The United Methodist Church is a global denomination, and our passion is for reaching the whole world for Christ and ministering to needs everywhere in the world.

The month of March continues the Lenten journey, and in most congregations this season affords a variety of mission opportunities. Our concern for both personal holiness and social holiness leads many of our congregations to host food pantries, soup kitchens, clothes closets, tutoring programs, and a variety of mission opportunities. United Methodists take the lead in efforts like Volunteers in Mission teams that clean up after hurricanes, rebuild damaged homes, and help people recover from disaster. March is a time to evaluate the effectiveness of these mission projects, to learn about additional social needs in our communities, and to explore new mission opportunities. These questions can help us shape our response to the gift of God's grace:

- Who are the overlooked persons in your community?
- What needs are going unmet?
- What strengths does your congregation have to offer?
- How can a deeper understanding of the Wesleyan Way of discipleship call you and your church to move beyond itself in ministry to others?

Our emphasis upon growth in personal and social holiness calls for for United Methodist people to stretch themselves in love and caring for others. Discipleship in the Wesleyan tradition is never just an individual concern; it is a compelling call to care for the whole of God's world.

As you and your congregation go deeper into the Lenten journey and as you seek to grow in personal and social holiness, spend time in Bible study using a text like Jesus' Parable of the Sheep and the Goats in Matthew 25:31–46. Reflect on these questions as an individual disciple and as a congregation:

- In what ways are we ministering to the least, the last, and the lost?
- Where in our community do we need to stand against unjust systems?
- What would Wesley's call to personal and social holiness mean for us today, in our lives and in our church?

Being a United Methodist Christian who stands in the Wesleyan tradition of discipleship does not let us escape such difficult questions. Essentially, we are a people who understand the individual and corporate need to grow in faith in God through Jesus Christ, and we understand our need to hold one another accountable in the Christian social community of the church in order to live out our faith both with other Christians and with all other people across the larger world. The month of March is a time to follow Jesus toward the cross, and it is a time to grow in our holiness.

April

John Wesley's Understanding of Sanctifying Grace and Christian Perfection

Henry H. Knight III

WHAT DOES IT MEAN for us to be created in the image of God? For John Wesley, the "image of God" has three interrelated dimensions. We reflect God's free agency in the *natural image*, which gives us understanding, freedom, and affections (or a disposition of the will). We reflect God's role in governing creation in the *political image*, our capacity for responsible stewardship. Most importantly, we reflect God's essential character in the *moral image*, which is love. God *is* love. "Accordingly," says Wesley, humanity as originally created was "full of love" as "the sole governing principle of . . . [all] . . . tempers, thoughts, words and actions" ("The New Birth," I.1).

Due to humanity's fall into sin, we no longer reflect that fullness of love. We have lost the moral image. Consequently, in our natural image we no longer have the freedom to love as God loves, but instead we have a disposition to put self and things we desire ahead of God and our neighbor. Likewise, in our political image we now misgovern creation, making selfish use of that for which God intended us to care.

The good news is this: God intends to restore us fully to the image in which we were created. It is for that purpose Christ came; it is for that purpose the Holy Spirit is at work. Restoring us to the fullness of love is, says Wesley, the essence of salvation: "a present deliverance from sin, a restoration of the soul to its primitive health, its original purity; a recovery of the divine nature" (*Farther Appeal to Men of Reason and Religion, Part I*, I.3).

Christian perfection is the goal of salvation. Of course, the word "perfection" can be for us a stumbling block. When Wesley uses the word, he does not mean an absolute perfection from which there can be no improvement. Nor does he mean freedom from errors of judgment or bodily weakness—we remain finite creatures. He also does not mean freedom from temptation (after all, even Jesus underwent temptation). Christian perfection does not mean that everything we do is in keeping with the will of God (what Wesley calls "involuntary transgressions" remain). What he *does* mean is this:

> Entire sanctification, or Christian perfection, is neither more nor less than pure love—love expelling sin and governing both the heart and life of a child of God (Letter to Walter Churchey, Feb. 21, 1771).

Only God can enable us to be once again the persons we were created to be. Wesley urges his Methodists to seek earnestly to be filled with God's love and to remain open and receptive to all that God may do in their lives each and every day through sanctifying grace. We can, he says, meet God in those places where God has promised to be: in the words of scripture, in the bread and cup at the Lord's Table, in prayer, and in the neighbor in need. Wesley believes we can all receive greater love than we have yet known, a love that leaves no room for sin in our hearts, and a life that death itself cannot keep us from enjoying through all eternity.

Hymn by Charles Wesley
Love Divine, All Loves Excelling

Love divine, all loves excelling, joy of heaven, to earth come down;
  Fix in us thy humble dwelling; all thy faithful mercies crown!
Jesus, thou art all compassion, pure, unbounded love thou art;
  Visit us with thy salvation; enter every trembling heart.

Breathe, O breathe thy loving Spirit into every troubled breast!
  Let us all in thee inherit; let us find that second rest.
Take away our bent to sinning; Alpha and Omega be;
  End of faith, as its beginning, set our hearts at liberty.

The United Methodist Hymnal, #384

April: A Time to Celebrate Easter and Grow in Grace

Bishop Coyner

THE MONTH OF APRIL often includes Easter Sunday and part of the Easter Season (which continues from Easter Sunday through the "Great Fifty Days" to Pentecost Sunday). A Wesleyan perspective on Easter includes a focus upon sanctifying grace and Christian perfection. This emphasis reminds us that Easter is not a one-day-a-year experience, but that new life in Christ is a growing, sustaining, expanding presence. April is a good time to emphasize that Easter is a complete liturgical season, and an Easter faith is a lifetime of growing in God's grace.

One way to teach about growing in grace is to ask long-time, faithful Christians in your congregation to testify in worship or in educational settings. Ask them to share their faith journeys, and their own lives will witness to God's ongoing and continuing work. Much of our U.S. culture tends toward instant gratification in everything, including religious experience. The Wesleyan model of discipleship offers a helpful corrective that faith is also a marathon experience of growing in God's grace over our whole lives.

It is helpful to note that the term "Christian perfection" does not mean being error-free, or perfectionism, but it does mean that God's grace perfects us in love. The whole Easter celebration reminds us that it is the living presence of Jesus Christ that guides us and helps us to grow into Christ's likeness.

The butterfly is a wonderful symbol of both Easter and the transforming, sanctifying grace of God. Perhaps your church will want to use this symbol to teach children about God's renewing love. The butterfly also can be a powerful visual for worship and a reminder that the Christian life is meant to be beautiful and not just a rigid set of moralisms. Opening our lives to the Spirit of God enables us to be perfected in love, in beauty, and in holiness. Such an image helps to overcome the fear that Christian Perfection is about perfectionism.

In the United States, we are blessed that Easter and spring coincide, so it is possible to celebrate the growth of flowers, the greening of the earth, and the freshness of spring weather as symbols of God's sanctifying grace bringing new life to our lives. In fact, growing a garden is an oft-used image of spiritual formation, as we focus upon opening our lives to God's grace in order to grow in the love of God. Consider this story about Thomas Merton:

> Merton told me once to quit trying so hard in prayer. He said: How does an apple ripen? It just sits in the sun. A small green apple cannot ripen in one night by tightening all its muscles, squinting its eyes and tightening its jaw in order to find itself the next morning miraculously large, red, ripe, and juicy beside its small green counterparts. Like the birth of a baby or the opening of a rose, the birth of the true self takes place in God's time. We must wait for God, we must be awake; we must trust in God's hidden action within us.

> *James Finney, from Merton's* Palace of Nowhere

MAY

John Wesley on the Means of Grace

Henry H. Knight III

JOHN WESLEY WAS FIRMLY COMMITTED to the Protestant principle that salvation is by grace alone. What he rejected was any depiction of grace where persons were simply passive recipients. Instead, he saw grace enabling and inviting us into a transforming relationship with God. We are to be active recipients, responding to God and remaining open to receive all that God offers us.

While God is free to meet us in extraordinary ways, Wesley believed God has promised to meet us in the means of grace. He defined "means of grace" as "outward signs, words, or actions ordained of God, and appointed for this end—to be the *ordinary* channels whereby he might convey . . . preventing, justifying, or sanctifying grace" ("Means of Grace," II.1). The means of grace are things we do or say that the Holy Spirit uses to enable our growth in the Christian life.

In describing means of grace, Wesley frequently distinguished between "works of piety" and "works of mercy." **Works of piety** are those means of grace that have God as their object. Among these are public and private prayer; the Lord's Supper; reading, hearing and mediating on scripture; and Christian conversation.

Prayer, said Wesley, is "the breath of our spiritual life" (*Explanatory Notes Upon the New Testament*, 1 Thess. 5:16). Just as breathing is necessary to our physical life, so is prayer to our life with God.

Wesley urged persons to use every opportunity to partake of the **Lord's Supper.** When we come to communion, he said, Jesus Christ "will meet you at his own table"

("On Working Out Our Own Salvation," II.4), bringing the very life of God to our souls.

Regarding **scripture**, Wesley noted that when Paul urges the Colossians to "Let the word of Christ dwell in you richly" he does not mean it should "make a short stay, or an occasional visit, but to take up its stated residence . . . so as to fill and govern the whole soul" (*Explanatory Notes Upon the New Testament*, Col. 3:16). Wesley applied this principle to scripture as a whole. As we read it and meditate upon it, God speaks to us through it, it dwells within us, and the word of Christ increasingly governs our hearts and lives.

Whether conferences with preachers, large society meetings, or smaller class and band meetings, **Christian conversation** was a constant feature of early Methodism. Wesley was convinced that when we talk about what it would mean for God's will to be done on earth as it is in heaven, God will work in our lives to enable us to be more faithful and loving.

Works of mercy have our neighbor as their object. Wesley urged Methodists to do good to all people, to their bodies as well as their souls. In his day, this included feeding the hungry, visiting the sick and those in prison, aiding the stranger, providing education and training, opposing evils such as the slave trade, and healing through medicine and prayer. Wesley insisted that it was not enough to do things for the poor; Methodists should get to know them through developing relationships with them. As they did, God would work through those relationships, and the works of mercy would be a means of grace for both.

It is in these and other means of grace that we find the presence and power of God that transforms our lives, enabling us ever more fully to love God and our neighbor as God has loved us.

Hymn by Charles Wesley
Long Have I Seemed to Serve Thee, Lord

Long have I seemed to serve thee, Lord,
    With unavailing pain;
Fasted, and prayed, and read thy word,
    And heard it preached in vain.

Oft did I with the assembly join,
    And near thine altar drew;
A form of godliness was mine,
    The power I never knew.

Here, in thine own appointed ways,
    I wait to learn thy will;
Silent I stand before thy face,
    And hear thee say, "Be still!"

A Collection of Hymns for the Use of the People called Methodists, 1780

May: A Time to Learn about the Means of Grace

Bishop Coyner

MANY CHURCHES CELEBRATE Confirmation Sunday sometime during the month of May as a part of the fifty-day Easter celebration, so this month is a good time to teach about the means of grace. The Wesleyan perspective on discipleship joins other Protestant churches in recognizing two sacraments: baptism and communion. The Protestant Reformation departed from Roman Catholicism by reducing the number of sacraments from seven to the two that the New Testament says Jesus "instituted" or commanded. Jesus taught us to "baptize in the name of the Father, Son, and Holy Spirit," and Jesus taught us when we share the bread and cup to "do this in remembrance of me."

The United Methodist Church celebrates baptism as the beginning of church membership, and so we baptize children with their parents or guardians professing vows of faith and promising to raise their children in the faith. When children are old enough to go through Confirmation, they become "professing members" who make their own faith promises to Christ and the Church. Persons can be baptized by any of the three uses of water—aspersion (sprinkling), effusion (pouring), or immersion (dunking)—because we understand that it is God's Spirit who baptizes us and not the amount of water. Likewise, in our church we celebrate Holy Communion with an open table whereby all who come seeking Christ are welcome. Normally baptism precedes receiving communion, but our church does not require that a person be baptized to receive, and we certainly do not require persons to be members of our church or of any church to receive. We regard both baptism and communion as "means of grace" whereby God reaches out to us and we respond in faith. (For more teaching material about our sacraments, *By Water and the Spirit* and *This Holy Mystery* are available as helpful study guides for your church.)

As you confirm youth into the faith, your church will have a teachable moment when you may explain the meaning of our sacraments as "sacred moments" when we believe that God is present in our lives. Confirmation is also a time to teach about the importance of church membership. Although we live in a culture in which many persons are reluctant to join institutions, church membership is a statement of faith and intentionality to live a life of Christian discipleship. It is more than just an institutional act; it is a declaration of one's commitment to Christ and to the Body of Christ, the Church.

Some churches find that Confirmation Sunday is a time for every member to recommit themselves to faithful membership and discipleship. As your church welcomes youth through confirmation or anyone else into membership, emphasize and celebrate the congregational response from the liturgy: "With you we renew our vows to uphold the church by our prayers, our presence, our gifts, and our service."

Ｊ Ｕ Π Ｅ

John Wesley's Stress on Connection in the Christian Life

Randy L. Maddox

WHAT IS THE ESSENCE OF "Methodism" as a distinctive part of the larger Christian family? Wesley's most common response to that question refused identifying a particular doctrine or set of worship practices, presenting Methodists instead as mainstream Christians who simply sought to experience and embody the fullness of the transforming impact of God's love in their lives (see *Character of a Methodist*). At the same time, if one watches carefully, a stress on the importance of *connexion* (as the British spell it) emerges repeatedly in Wesley's accounts of Methodism.

For example, Wesley's various historical accounts of Methodism begin not with the deepened stress on grace after Aldersgate, but with the gathering of a small community at Oxford to support one another in pursuit of more vital Christian life. Conversely, when assessing George Whitefield's ministry, Wesley's strongest criticism was not his preaching of predestination, but that Whitefield did not follow up his powerful preaching by organizing those who responded into supportive groups: "They had no Christian connexion with each other, nor were ever taught to watch over each other's souls. So that if any fell into lukewarmness, or even into sin, he had none to lift him up" ("The Late Work of God in North America," I.7). It was this vital contribution of connection to spiritual growth that Wesley had in mind when he insisted, "there is no holiness but social holiness."

For all of its benefits, if one stresses only such connection to a small group, there is danger of insularity and bigotry. Wesley recognized this danger and suggested that the best counter lay in a further layer of connection—with the larger Christian family. His sermon "Catholic Spirit" is a classic call for embracing the full spectrum of the Christian community in fellowship and honest dialogue. Importantly, he grounded this call in the recognition that, as humans, we ought always to be open to the possibility that we could gain further insight into Christian truth through encounters with those who differ from us (and offer them insight as well). Ideally, such a connection would draw us all toward more adequate understanding and greater consensus.

Implicit in the sermon "Catholic Spirit" is a third important dimension of connection for Wesley. He sought to strengthen cooperative ministry among the wings of the evangelical revival in England. Wesley recognized that the church exists for more than just the edification of believers; it is called to participate in God's redemptive mission to all persons. He also sensed that a broad connection with other Christians enhances effectiveness in this role, both because it spreads the labor and because it embodies the reconciliation that we proclaim.

In some of Wesley's last sermons he directs attention to yet another important dimension of connection—our integral relationship with the whole creation and our accountability for its care (see particularly "The General Deliverance"). Wesley's emphasis on this point led to Methodists being strongly associated with concern for animal rights in England at the turn of the nineteenth century!

While other dimensions could be distinguished, the preceding is sufficient to make the point that when we describe United Methodism as a "connectional church" we have in mind more than just a particular polity. We are inheritors of Wesley's appreciation for the vital contributions of connection within the life and work of the church.

Hymn by Charles Wesley
All Praise to Our Redeeming Lord

All praise to our redeeming Lord, who joins us by his grace,
And bids us, each to each restored, together seek his face.

He bids us build each other up; and, gathered into one,
To our high calling's glorious hope we hand in hand go on.

The gift which he on one bestows, we all delight to prove,
The grace through every vessel flows in purest streams of love.

The United Methodist Hymnal, #554

June: A Time to Celebrate Our Connectional Church

Bishop Coyner

IN MANY PARTS OF THE United States, the month of June is time for the yearly meeting of the annual conference. This gathering of clergy and lay members from the churches in a geographic region is a reminder that our United Methodist Church is a "connectional church," which means that every local church belongs to a larger entity. Wesley's teaching that "the world is my parish" provides the foundation for our United Methodist understanding that the local church is also a part of a global church connection.

In addition to participating fully in your annual conference, your local church may teach and demonstrate this connection by some of these activities:

- Pray each Sunday for other United Methodist congregations in your area, including the names of those pastors and churches in your prayers.
- Consider relating to a United Methodist congregation in Africa, Europe, or the Philippines as a partner, eventually even visiting that congregation.
- Pay your apportionments (shared giving) in full as a demonstration of your church's participation in the global ministry of our denomination.
- Learn about missionaries from your annual conference and pray for them.
- Display maps of the world that illustrate the location of United Methodist ministries with which you are connected.
- Conduct small-group studies about the global mission of the church.

One of the temptations of American and similar cultures is to become selfish and localized in our concerns, rather than responding faithfully to God who "so loved the world that he gave his only Son that whoever believes in him should not perish but have everlasting life" (John 3:16). Some have described the danger of changing John Wesley's famous teaching, "The world is my parish" into the selfish perspective, "My parish is my world." As United Methodists, we struggle to be faithful to God both in our local congregations and in our global ministries. The month of June, including annual conference time (or in whatever month your annual conference meets), is a reminder of our call to minister beyond the walls of our local congregations.

Annual conference time is also an opportunity to learn about our Wesleyan understanding of "conferencing." John Wesley and his followers were called "Methodists" for their methodical way of organizing, and it is still true that we tend to have many committees and many meetings. However, the theological purpose of those meetings is to "conference" with one another and with God. Before your clergy and lay members go to annual conference, and before you have your next local church meetings this month, remind yourselves that we gather for such meetings in order to follow the model of the early disciples who gathered in the Upper Room praying and waiting for God's Spirit to empower and guide them (Acts 2). Our meetings in the United Methodist Church are intended to be more than meetings; they are meant to be times of praying, conferencing, and receiving God's power for our ministry in our local communities and for our connectional ministries around the world.

J U LY

John Wesley's Call to Be an "Altogether Christian"

F. Douglas Powe Jr.

THE TENDENCY OF MOST CHRISTIANS, in Wesley's day and today, is to judge the seriousness of their commitment by the frequency of their attendance in church services or their participation on mission trips. While Wesley affirmed the value of such activities, he recognizes that they can become mere formalities. The heart of the early Methodist revival was the insistence that both God's expectation and our spiritual need point toward something much deeper than such outward matters. Wesley framed this deeper reality in the call to be "altogether Christian," rather than just "almost Christian." In a 1741 sermon, he articulates the difference in these terms:

> The great question of all, then, still remains. Is the love of God shed abroad in your heart? Can you cry out, "My God and my all"? Do you desire nothing but him? Are you happy in God? Is he your glory, your delight, your crown of rejoicing? And is this commandment written in your heart, "that he who loveth God love his brother also"? Do you then love your neighbor as yourself? Do you love every man, even your enemies, even the enemies of God, as your own soul? ("The Almost Christian," II.9).

Note first that Wesley does not let us off the hook by equating love for God with merely praying or reading the Bible; the expectation is a heart *filled* with the love of God. Wesley writes, "[one's] heart is ever crying out, 'whom have I in heaven but thee? And there is none upon earth that I desire beside thee'" (Ibid., II.1). Such a love encompasses every part of our being. God becomes our focal point, and we desire to be perfected in our love for God. As noted in an earlier essay, this is not a desire for freedom from our human frailty, but a longing to embody dynamically the heart and mind of Christ.

Note secondly how Wesley assumes that, as we mature daily in our love of God, this materity should translate into loving our neighbors differently. In particular, we must understand that every person in the world is our neighbor—even those who have caused us harm in some manner. Loving those close to us or like us is fairly easy, but an altogether Christian loves those whom we perceive as our enemies (Ibid., II.2.).

Wesley is setting the bar quite high! He recognizes clearly at this point the danger of mediocrity when mere outward formality reduces Christian discipleship. However, it is important to stress that over the years of the revival he came to recognize equally the danger of driving honest seekers to despair by focusing exclusively on the ultimate ideal. Consider his seasoned words in a 1787 sermon:

> I would be far from quenching the smoking flax, from discouraging those that serve God in a low degree. But I would not wish them to stop here: I would encourage them to come up higher, without thundering hell and damnation in their ears, without condemning the way wherein they were, telling them it is the way that leads to destruction. I will endeavor to point out to them what is in every respect a more excellent way ("More Excellent Way," §7).

In this pastoral balance, Wesley's fundamental conviction remains clear: what God graciously offers, and what we should continually desire, is to become *altogether* Christian.

Hymn by Charles Wesley

Jesus, Lord, We Look to Thee

By thy reconciling love every stumbling block remove;
Each to each unite, endear; come, and spread thy banner here.

Make us of one heart and mind, gentle, courteous, and kind,
Lowly, meek, in thought and word, altogether like our Lord.

Let us for each other care, each the other's burdens bear;
To thy church the pattern give, show how true believers live.

The United Methodist Hymnal, #562

July: A Time to Live as Altogether Christians

Bishop Coyner

BOTH CHARLES AND JOHN WESLEY offended members of the Anglican Church by their challenge to move beyond being "Almost Christian" to being "Altogether Christians" who put their faith into practice. The month of July is a time in the United States when being an "Altogether Christian" is not easy. Summertime often brings a drop in faithful worship attendance as people focus upon their own leisure activities. Additionally, the Fourth of July holiday confronts us with the challenge of being faithful Christians in the midst of patriotic holiday expressions that can become nationalistic. How does one keep the balance of being an "Altogether Christian" in the midst of such times?

Many churches in the northern hemisphere find that summer months afford opportunity for different styles and times of worship and study. July is a good time to host special Sunday events that could include a dialogue about the appropriate role of patriotism or a focus upon balancing family life and faith in the midst of summer schedules. July is a time to thank God for religious freedom, but also to include a study of Paul's letter to the Galatians in which he challenged them (and us) to use and not misuse their freedoms.

The month of July is a good time to plan or to engage in mission trips that remind church-goers to put their faith into action. Many churches sponsor youth going to church camps, and having the youth report on their experiences of living in a Christian communities at camp can be another way to promote discussion about being "Altogether Christians." Perhaps your church can offer opportunities during July to help your people reflect on these questions, either in sermons or in small-group discussions:

- Have I given my whole life over to Christ?
- If I were to measure my faith, would I consider myself an "Almost Christian" or an "Altogether Christian"?
- What is holding me back from being truly an "Altogether Christian"?

In true Wesleyan style, these are questions to be raised by the preacher, but they are questions best explored in small groups or other places of trusted Christian conversation. They also are questions to explore with regard to our nations, perhaps using this prayer from the *Book of Worship* (#442):

Almighty God, you rule all the peoples of the earth.

Inspire the minds of women and men to whom you have committed the responsibility of government and leadership in the nations of the world.

Give to them the vision of truth and justice, that by their counsel all nations and peoples may work together.

Give to the people of our country zeal for justice and strength of forbearance, that we may use our liberty in accordance with your gracious will.

Forgive our shortcomings as a nation; purify our hearts to see and love the truth.

We pray these things through Jesus Christ. Amen.

August

John Wesley on Holistic Mission

Randy L. Maddox

ON SEVERAL OCCASIONS, John Wesley identified the distinctive concern of the early Methodist revival as reclaiming for the larger Christian family a focus on personal holiness, nurtured in community. This emphasis, explored in earlier entries, aligned Methodism with other "pietist" movements in Europe and North America. Critics of these movements sometimes charge that their focus on the inward life displaced concern for engaging the pressing needs in our world. Whatever the case in other settings, this charge cannot be pinned on Wesley and Methodism. Consider one of Wesley's earliest responses to questions about the agenda of the revival:

> This is the religion we long to see established in the world, a religion of love and joy and peace, having its seat in the heart, in the inmost soul, but ever showing itself by its fruits, continually springing forth, not only in all innocence . . . but likewise in every kind of beneficence, in spreading virtue and happiness all around it ("Earnest Appeal to Men of Reason and Religion", §4).

The first thing to see in this statement is that inner renewal and engagement with the world are integrally connected. Deepened experience of the love of God renders one *more* likely to reach out in love to others, not less. Conversely, as we minister to and with those in need around us, allowing the love of God to flow through us serves not only to meet their need but also to deepen our renewal—a point Wesley made by stressing works of mercy as a crucial "means of grace."

Note as well the balance that Wesley highlighted in authentic engagement with the world. There is not only the concern to avoid fault (that might lead one to separate from the world!), but also the desire to cultivate the well-being of others. This balance was so central that Wesley built it into the foundation of Methodist life—the General Rules. The first of the rules was "Do no harm"; the second, "Do as much good as you can for others." The remaining rule about regular participation in the means of grace undergirded the first two by nurturing the heart from which these actions spring as fruit.

Review of the General Rules will reveal that they focus mainly on *personal* social justice (do no harm) and *service* to those in need (do good). There is little emphasis on "social witness," or the attempt to influence broader society to change structures that inflict harm. But this should not be seen as principled opposition to such a focus, reflecting instead the small size and limited influence of early Methodism. As the movement grew and Wesley recognized that they might have some political influence, he exhorted his Methodist followers to add their voices (and names on petitions) to such agendas as calling for abolition of the slave trade.

As Methodism continued to grow, gaining political prominence in some settings, the element of social witness became a central emphasis in mission to the world. Wesley would surely have welcomed this development—as long as it does not displace the other dimensions of mission embodied in the General Rules. Alongside our advocacy for change on the part of governments, corporations, and the like, those who stand in the Methodist tradition of holistic mission should never forget to focus upon our own actions, as well as and upon faithful participation in the means of grace that nurture deep and abiding concern for others.

Hymn by Charles Wesley

Give Me the Faith Which Can Remove

I would the precious time redeem, and longer live for this alone,
  To spend and to be spent for them who have not yet my Savior known;
Fully on these my mission prove, and only breathe, to breathe thy love.

Enlarge, inflame, and fill my heart with boundless charity divine,
  So shall I all my strength exert, and love them with a zeal like thine,
And lead them to thy open side, the sheep for whom the Shepherd died.

The United Methodist Hymnal, #650

August: A Time to Teach Social Mission

Bishop Coyner

THE YEAR 2008 is the hundredth anniversary of the first adoption of a Social Creed by the predecessors to The United Methodist Church. The Social Principles have been a part of our *Book of Discipline* because of our Wesleyan emphasis upon "spreading scriptural holiness" across every continent. Part of our Methodist revival heritage is a profound belief that personal salvation and social mission go hand-in-hand.

Your local church can teach this emphasis by providing a series of adult class lessons on the Social Principles. Study guides are available from the General Board of Church and Society, and their website includes background information to help teach about our Social Creed and Social Principles. You may want to remind people that the Social Principles are prophetic in nature—speaking for the church (as revised and adopted every four years by General Conference), but also speaking to the church to challenge us into dialogue about the important social issues of our day. It might be helpful to include Our Social Creed in times of worship during August:

We believe in God, Creator of the world; and in Jesus Christ, the Redeemer of creation. We believe in the Holy Spirit, through whom we acknowledge God's gifts; and we repent of our sin in misusing these gifts to idolatrous ends.

We affirm the natural world as God's handiwork and dedicate ourselves to its preservation, enhancement, and faithful use by humankind.

We joyfully receive for ourselves and others the blessings of community, sexuality, marriage, and the family.

We commit ourselves to the rights of men, women, children, youth, young adults, the aging, and people with disabilities; to improvement of the quality of life; and to the rights and dignity of all persons.

We believe in the right and duty of persons to work for the glory of God and the good of themselves and others and in the protection of their welfare in so doing; in the rights to property as a trust from God, collective bargaining, and responsible consumption; and in the elimination of economic and social distress.

We dedicate ourselves to peace throughout the world, to the rule of justice and law among nations, and to individual freedom for all people of the world.

We believe in the present and final triumph of God's Word in human affairs and gladly accept our commission to manifest the life of the gospel in the world. Amen (*The Book of Discipline*, ¶166).

Social mission is a passion for all United Methodists who understand that our Christian discipleship is never just an individual quest. Sharing this creed in public worship during August may help your congregation remember this lesson.

SEPTEMBER

The Wesley Brothers on Knowledge and Vital Piety

Sarah Heaner Lancaster

THE WESLEYS UNDERSTOOD that Christian life should involve both learning and devotion. From an early age, John and Charles received excellent education, first from their mother, Susanna, and in later life from formal university study. They knew that learning could add to their love for God, so study took its place alongside prayer, fasting, Holy Communion, and other spiritual practices as an important component of disciplined life before God. Although John Wesley sometimes called himself a "man of one book" because of his reliance on the Bible, he was widely read, and he understood the value of studying history, logic, and philosophy for understanding Christian faith. He used the search for truth in any form in service of God, and he read both theology and classical literature into advanced age.

The phrase "knowledge and vital piety" comes from a hymn by Charles Wesley that was sung at the opening of the Kingswood School for children. In founding this school, John Wesley wanted to provide for children an education that would bring together intellectual understanding and religious devotion. Still in operation today, the Kingswood School continues to seek this goal for its students. The idea that early formation would result in lifelong holistic growth in faith is one that has remained important for education in the Methodist tradition. For this reason, Methodists were among the earliest and strongest supporters of Sunday schools.

John Wesley wanted the same kind of holistic formation for Methodist preachers. Wesley expected them to lead a life of holiness and to promote holiness in others, but they were not equally educated. In order that Methodist preachers might be as learned as possible, John Wesley provided them with material for study and expected them to spend time every day reading. He selected some of his own sermons to serve as guides for their preaching, and he published commentaries on the Bible to introduce the preachers to biblical scholarship that they would not have had access to otherwise. In addition, he collected, edited, and abridged many works in theology into a Christian library of fifty volumes. Publishing houses, colleges, universities, and seminaries have carried forward Wesley's commitment to education by making theological scholarship accessible and affordable.

Methodists preached assurance of God's love, and they sought to help people have a genuine encounter with God that would provide the foundation for ongoing relationship with God. Piety was *vital* when God's love for them enlivened Christians so that their practices were not empty displays, but instead became means of grace that enabled them to grow in love. The emphasis on personal experience did have its danger. John Wesley warned against "enthusiasm," which involved a kind of unthinking emotionalism. One of the reasons for valuing sound learning was that it could help interpret experience. However, rationalism was just as dangerous as emotionalism because it could lead to reliance on one's own powers rather than on God. So again, the combination of knowledge and vital piety was crucial for keeping the balance that would lead to genuine growth in faith.

United Methodists honor this heritage when we seek both solid understanding informed by the best resources we have available and deeply spiritual lives formed by regular participation in the means of grace.

Hymn by Charles Wesley
I Want a Principle Within

I want a principle within of watchful, godly fear,
A sensibility of sin, a pain to feel it near.
I want the first approach to feel of pride or wrong desire,
To catch the wandering of my will, and quench the kindling fire.

Almighty God of truth and love, to me thy power impart;
The mountain from my soul remove, the hardness from my heart.
O may the least omission pain my reawakened soul,
And drive me to that blood again, which makes the wounded whole.

The United Methodist Hymnal, #410

September: A Time to Grow in Knowledge and Vital Piety

Bishop Coyner

JOHN WESLEY DECLARED that we in the Methodist revival tradition "bring together those two so long divided: knowledge and vital piety." By that phrase, he meant that faith always yearns for increased learning and that education should illuminate our acts of worship and piety. Some people say our United Methodist Church is a "thinking church"—not to imply that other denominations do not think, but to emphasize that we in the tradition of John Wesley affirm the essential need for education. Thus it is that the followers of John Wesley have started schools, colleges, universities, and seminaries wherever we have taught the gospel. Africa University is perhaps the latest and best example of our desire to promote both knowledge and vital piety, or education and faith.

Nearly every United Methodist Church has a Sunday school or other forms of educational classes for children, youth, and adults. Why? Because we affirm that a faithful person is also a thinking, learning, and growing person. Faith is not limited to a set of doctrines or assents to which one concurs but never challenges or debates. Faith includes education such as Bible study, small-group sharing, discussion, and growth.

Often the month of September in the United States is a time when churches offer "Rally Days" or other starts of the Sunday school year. Such a special day is a time for the pastor to assume her or his role as teacher and to include teaching the importance of being a "thinking church" and "thinking Christian." Since so many people in our world (and even some long-time members in our churches) are biblically illiterate, it may be helpful to offer beginning Bible study classes to help persons get started on the road to an educated faith.

We United Methodists believe that Bible study is also informed by the traditions of the faith, the use of reason, and the experience of the Christian community (not just individualistic experience) in knowing God's will. Modern followers of Wesley have described this holistic understanding of theology and learning as the Wesley Quadrilateral of scripture, tradition, reason, and experience. While not a term that John Wesley used himself, the *Discipline* summarizes the central point of the Quadrilateral in this way: "Wesley believed that the living core of the Christian faith was revealed in scripture, illumined by tradition, vivified in personal experience, and confirmed by reason." Beginning with the 1972 *Book of Discipline* and revised in 1988 to clarify its meaning, this teaching about the Wesley Quadrilateral is included in the section of the *Discipline* entitled "Our Theological Task." That section is worth studying!

Sarah Heaner Lancaster has described the use of the Wesley Quadrilateral this way:

The word "quadrilateral" does not mean "equilateral" (where all sides would be treated equally), and the current statement makes clear that Scripture has primary place in theological reflection. The other three, though, have essential roles to play. The point of approaching theological reflection as described in the *Discipline* is not to choose one as decisive over the others, but to find how they mutually inform us of what God would have us understand.

That focus upon faith seeking understanding is a part of our Wesleyan heritage. Celebrate it during the month of September.

OCTOBER

John Wesley on Stewardship

Sarah Heaner Lancaster

JOHN WESLEY'S UNDERSTANDING of stewardship was rooted in his larger theological understanding of our relationship with God. Everything that we have comes from God. We did not bring our own existence into being, we do not cause the growth that provides the food that we eat, and we do not make the raw materials that we use for our work. God gives not only these basic requirements for life, but also the fullness of life that we call "salvation." It is easy to forget the many ways in which God provides for us and to think that we ourselves are solely responsible for what we are and what we have. Giving back to God is a way of reminding ourselves that God is the source of all the things we value.

Just as life itself comes to us as gift from God, the way we use that life is a gift back to God. That is why cultivating inward and outward holiness matters. The way we respond to words spoken to us in anger, the way we spend our time, or the attention that we pay to others can be gifts to God of our very selves when they reflect the mind of Christ.

All of this was important to Wesley, but he had a particular interest in getting Christians to reflect on how they earn and spend money. The reason for paying so much attention to this subject is that money has a huge impact on quality of life, both for ourselves and for others. Wesley famously offered the advice, "Gain all you can, save all you can, and give all you can." What may be less well known is that Wesley also talked at length about how to carry out this advice.

Wesley put restrictions on the way we *gain* all we can. Earning money was discouraged if it came at the expense of our own health, whether physical or spiritual. This caution rules out gaining all one can through "workaholism" or through any means that leads us to cheat, lie, or in any way violate the standards that Christians ought to hold. Nor should we earn money at the expense of another person's physical or spiritual health. The business we conduct should be fitting to a life dedicated to God.

Similarly, the way we *save* all we can also matters. Wesley's idea runs much deeper than getting a good deal or buying things on sale. What we buy matters as much as what we pay for it. For Wesley, saving meant avoiding any expense that was simply for our own pleasure, rather than for taking care of a legitimate need. He understood that indulging our desires could lead us away from God. He also understood that spending money on unnecessary items left less for us to give to others. The point of saving is not hoarding; it is giving.

To *give* all we can is to reflect God's own generosity and thus to participate in God's work. We are to manage our money and property to be able to use it for God's purposes. If we think about the use of money as a spiritual discipline, then we can see that the point is not to give away what we think is extra. The point is to play our role in distributing God's resources equitably, not denying our own needs, but seeing the needs of others to be as legitimate as our own.

Hymn by Charles Wesley
Father, Into Thy Hands Alone

Father, into Thy hands alone I have my all restored;

My all, Thy property I own, the steward of the Lord.
Determined all Thy will to obey, Thy blessings I restore;
Give, Lord, or take Thy gifts away; I praise Thee evermore.

Wesley Hymns, Lillenas Publishing, 1982, #97

Alternate hymn selection:

Hymn by Joachim Lange, Translated by John Wesley
O God, What Offering Shall I Give?

O God, what offering shall I give to Thee, the Lord of earth and skies?
  My spirit, soul, and flesh receive, a holy, living sacrifice.
Small as it is, 'tis all my store; more should'st Thou have, if I had more.

Hymnal of The Methodist Episcopal Church, 1878, #474

October: A Time to Grow in Stewardship and Generosity

Bishop Coyner

MANY CHURCHES USE the month of October to conduct financial drives to underwrite their church budgets for the next year. While such fundraising efforts are laudable, a more Wesleyan approach would include an emphasis upon teaching stewardship and generosity. We do not ask our United Methodist people to give to support the church budget; we ask them to give out of a sense of gratitude to God.

Some church experts have noted that asking our members to give merely to support a church budget has limited results. Teaching people to give out of generous hearts, perhaps teaching the Biblical concept of the tithe (where we are invited to give a tithe or ten percent of our income), has almost unlimited possibilities. Generosity grows as one's income grows, and many generous United Methodists give far more than their share of a church budget or even just a tithe.

In many parts of the world, especially in the southern hemisphere, the call to give the offering during worship results in clapping, dancing, and a joyous response to God. By contrast, in many churches in Europe and North America, the offering time looks more often like a time of bill paying, long faces, and guilty consciences. Too often, the fall financial drive adds to this sense of joyless giving, and the emphasis upon loyalty to the church as an institution seems to have diminishing results—especially with young adults who want to be a part of a cause and to make a difference with their giving.

The Wesleyan emphasis upon perceiving all of life as a gift from God, along with the call to live in what Randy Maddox has called "responsible grace," may be an old word that congregations may hear in new ways as they seek to be faithful in the twenty-first century. How can you apply this to your church? You could consider having a true stewardship drive during October in which you teach stewardship and generosity and ask people to estimate their giving to God and then work to produce a budget based upon those results. Your church might consider using an approach like a Consecration Sunday (as taught by Herb Miller) with its emphasis upon stewardship rather than budget fundraising. You might also begin teaching stewardship to the children of the congregation, helping them to develop life-long habits of generosity.

October is a time to focus upon the Wesley understanding of stewardship and generosity. It is about so much more than money, but money does become one expression of our gratitude to God. The German hymn that John Wesley translated, "Jesus, Thy Boundless Love To Me," says it well:

> Jesus, Thy boundless love to me
> No thought can reach, no tongue declare;
> Unite my thankful heart with Thee
> And reign without a rival there.
> To Thee alone, dear Lord, I live;
> Myself to Thee, dear Lord, I give.

ΠOVEMBER

John Wesley on Mutuality
in Mission

F. Douglas Powe Jr.

ONE OF THE MOST UNFORTUNATE divides that separate people in the church today is the split between those who equate mission with proclaiming the gospel and those who focus mission on concern for social justice. The tendency of many is to present a forced choice: either you are concerned with evangelism or you are concerned with social justice. I believe that our Wesleyan tradition offers a more helpful third option—mutuality in mission.[3]

John Wesley hands down several dimensions of mutuality in mission to us, though we must recognize that his own appreciation for these grew over time. For example, one of the reasons that Wesley wanted to come to North America was to evangelize the Native Americans. At the outset of this journey, he conceived of mission as moving in one direction only—him taking the gospel to those who lacked it. As he returned from America, a chastened Wesley reflected in his *Journal* on January 29, 1738, "What have I learned myself in the meantime? Why (what I the least of all suspected), that I who went to America to convert others, was never myself converted to God." Here Wesley begins to understand that God is the true agent of all mission work and that when we participate in God's mission we often gain as much insight from those whom we approach as we are able, through God's grace, to share

[3]Rena Youcam, the Missiologist-in-residence at Saint Paul School of Theology, has delineated the concept of mutuality in a paper, "Mission and the Global Nature of the Church," presented at a United Methodist Consultation on the Global Nature of the Church, May, 2006.

with them. Evangelistic mission at its best will always be open to this mutuality.

Wesley came to a similar understanding concerning the dimension of mission focused on social service. Ministry to those who were in prison was a central part of the commitments of the early Oxford Methodists, but they framed this ministry in a unilateral direction. There was little sense that the Oxford Methodists expected to benefit themselves from the time spent with the prisoners. By contrast, this became a central emphasis of Wesley in his later years. He insisted that works of mercy were vital for Methodists to practice, not just because of how they benefited others, but because they were a "means of grace" that nourished the benefactor as well. At least they can be so if we enter into a mutual relationship with those in need. That is why Wesley insisted in his sermon "On Visiting the Sick" that his Methodist people do more than just send aid to the sick (in body or soul); they should also *visit* them in person.

One needs to highlight another dimension of Wesley's seasoned wisdom about mutuality mission. The early ministry to prisoners at Oxford could be understood as merely instrumental in purpose—addressing physical needs *in order* to win a hearing for the gospel. In later years Wesley was clear that concern for physical, social, and justice issues was integral to Christian ministry. Following the model of Christ, we are to minister to all who are in need, and simply because of their need! (See "Sermon on the Mount IV," §III.7). At the same time, precisely because he understood ministry in truly mutual terms, Wesley could insist that it was both unfaithful and unloving to minister only to people's physical needs, neglecting to convey to them God's offer of gracious transformation of the spiritual dimensions of their lives as well (see "On Visiting the Sick," §I.5 & §II.4).

This model of mutuality in ministry, in all of its dimensions, is a precious part of our heritage. It calls us to reject the common divisions along party lines (evangelism vs. social justice) and to enter into every form of mission open to experiencing how God seeks to transform us as well as how God may work through us in transforming others.

Hymn by Charles Wesley

A Charge to Keep I Have

A charge to keep I have, a God to glorify,
A never-dying soul to save, and fit it for the sky.

To serve the present age, my calling to fulfill;
O may it all my powers engage to do my Master's will!

The United Methodist Hymnal, #413

November: A Time to Give Thanks and to Celebrate Our Missions

Bishop Coyner

GIVING TO MISSIONS and engaging in missions are a part of our DNA as United Methodists. Nearly every local congregation is engaged in local mission work, including everything from a food pantry, to a clothing closet, to a counseling center, to relief efforts, and certainly to Thanksgiving offerings for missions. Most of our United Methodist churches have sent Volunteers in Mission (VIM) work teams or have engaged directly in other types of hands-on experiences of being in mission work to and with others.

What is the source of this "missions DNA" in our United Methodist churches? Clearly, it arises from the first Methodist people, led by the Wesley brothers and their Holy Club of students at Oxford, who saw that the Christian faith always involves caring for others. As noted in the study material by Douglas Powe, this original urge toward mission work was "missions to" the other person, but it grew into "missions with" the other person. Another way to express this difference is to say that we United Methodists today do not just practice charity, but we also work for an end to oppression, hunger, and pain in the world. Why? Because we have a profound belief that the God who "so loved the world that he gave his only Son" (John 3:16) is the same God who sends us forth to love the world and to seek justice, mercy, and love for all. Our momentum towards missions, then, arises from our gratitude to God.

In order for November to be a time of Thanksgiving and emphasis on our missions, it will be helpful to offer hands-on experiences in giving and sharing. Simply receiving an offering for Thanksgiving or a designated offering for missions will not be enough to teach the Wesleyan model. Look for options that allow your congregation to be directly involved, perhaps working in a soup kitchen, taking a turn helping at a homeless shelter, or collecting and delivering food goods to a food pantry in the area.

Children can learn at an early age to be thankful, generous, and caring for others. The Parable of the Last Judgment in Matthew 25 allows for some dramatic reading and acting about the sheep and the goats that are separated based on "caring for the least of these." Some churches have involved children in a "noisy buckets" offering each Sunday of November. Children—even very young children—take small metal buckets and roam through the congregation to collect change. Then they empty those small buckets into a large metal bucket in the front of the church. Using metal buckets allows the sound of giving to be heard. Oftentimes the children will go through the congregation together, bringing a whole line of buckets to each person to receive their gifts. The noisy and generous response can add to the learning experience as people give repeatedly to each child.

November is also a good time to hear reports from previous mission trips and to recruit for upcoming trips. Having those reports set in a context of Thanksgiving and working for justice is an excellent way to teach the Wesleyan model of mutuality in mission. Nearly every person who reports about such a mission trip will share something like, "I went on this trip to give to others, but I received so much more." Hearing such reports of mutuality in mission will help to reinforce our DNA about missions.

DECEMBER

John Wesley on Prevenient Grace

Sarah Heaner Lancaster

THE WORD "PREVENIENT" comes from two Latin words that together mean "coming before." To say that grace is prevenient, then, is to say that God's grace comes to us before anything we do on our part to try to gain it. Grace, which is best understood as God's power and presence in our lives, is already at work in us to draw us to God even before we knowingly respond.

All of us are born needing God to be present and at work in us to bring us to the fullness of life that God has to offer. God begins to address this condition before we are even aware of it. One of the reasons United Methodists baptize infants is to demonstrate that both this human need and God's gracious fulfillment of that need are present from the beginning of our lives. Sometimes Wesley used the phrase "prevenient grace" to refer to this early work of God, and he used other phrases (such as justifying grace and sanctifying grace) to refer to other aspects of God's work. When he speaks of it in this way, Wesley could describe prevenient grace as available to every human being, making us aware of God, drawing us to God, helping us know right from wrong, and bringing forth our earliest responses to God's love.

The word "prevenient" can also describe the way that Wesley thought about every aspect of grace, even when he called it "justifying" or "sanctifying." God's grace comes before anything we do, regardless of the kind of work it accomplishes in us. Grace makes us capable of responding to God. It shows us where we fall short of what God intends for us. It calls us to repentance for our sin. It helps us to become increasingly Christ-like. It fills us with love for God and love for neighbor. Wesley can describe grace in other ways for these situations, but in every case, God's love comes before and calls forth our response.

Thinking of grace as prevenient in this broader sense reminds us that God empowers us at every step along the way of salvation. When we affirm with the Apostle Paul that we are justified by faith, we recognize that God's grace makes that faith possible. It is never simply up to us to choose or decide to be in relationship with God. Before we open ourselves, God has already been reaching out to draw us into that relationship. Similarly, we never do good works simply on our own. God empowers us to act in love so that all our efforts are rooted in God's grace. It is certainly possible to resist the promptings of grace, but when we do cooperate as we should, we acknowledge that God has prepared the way for us to follow.

At the heart of the Wesleyan understanding of prevenient grace, then, is recognition of God's initiative to reach out to us and of our continual dependence on God's support to become the people that God created us to be. God's action anticipates, invites, and enables our reaction. We may trust that God is always ahead of us, making us ready so that we may turn to the God who is already there to receive us.

Hymn by Charles Wesley

Thy Ceaseless, Unexhausted Love

Thou ceaseless, unexhausted love, unmerited and free,
Delights our evil to remove, and help our misery.

Thou waitest to be gracious still; Thou dost with sinners bear,
That, saved, we may Thy goodness feel and all Thy grace declare.

Hymnal of The Methodist Episcopal Church, 1878, #317

December: A Time to Celebrate the Christmas Gift of God's Grace

Bishop Coyner

THE SEASON OF Advent and Christmas is a joyous time in all of our United Methodist churches, and yet it affords some special challenges for us to teach a Wesleyan understanding of this gift of Christ without falling into the consumerism and crassness of our culture. While much of the world is focusing upon the exchange of gifts, our Wesleyan values remind us that the coming of Christ is a sign of God's prevenient grace.

How can we celebrate Christmas as United Methodists in an authentic and helpful way? Certainly, any celebration begins with the acknowledgment that God loved us first. Before we ever knew or earned God's love, God loved us first and demonstrated that love through the sending of Jesus Christ into the world. Therefore, our music, our sermons, our Sunday school lessons, and our personal devotions need to focus upon remembering how God's love surrounded our lives even before we responded. "While we were yet sinners" is the way Paul expresses this truth in Romans 5. He indicates that God's love came to us before we did anything to deserve it.

One way for congregations to celebrate this true meaning of Christmas is to focus upon giving to others who may or may not deserve our gifts. Everything from mitten trees, to gifts for needy families, to Christmas caroling for homebound persons can be signs of sharing God's love with others.

Some churches have started offering "Christmas Bible School" for children during December as a way of allowing parents to run errands (even Christmas shopping) while the children spend an evening each week at church learning the true meaning of Christmas, practicing a Christmas play or songs, and then sharing a worship time with their parents just before Christmas. Such a Christmas Bible School can be a wonderful outreach to the community, too, and it can lead naturally into an invitation to join the congregation for Advent and Christmas Eve worship.

On an individual level, December is a time for personal devotions that focus upon remembering and looking back upon our lives to see how God's grace has been evident in the ways, circumstances, and people who have blessed us and moved us toward God. For many persons, that will be recognition that Jesus was indeed "born at night" or at least born into the darkness of our world and our lives. The Gospels tell of a nighttime birth, which reminds us that the gift of God's grace comes into the darkness of our lives to offer light, hope, and love. As Isaiah declares, "The people walking in darkness have seen a great light" (Isaiah 9:2). Perhaps December is a time to remember with gratitude how God's prevenient grace has come to us as a light in our darkness.

December is truly a month to celebrate the Christmas Gift of God's Grace.

ADDITIONAL SUGGESTED RESOURCES

Chilcote, Paul Wesley. *Praying in the Wesleyan Spirit*. Nashville: Upper Room Books, 2001.

_____. *Recapturing the Wesleys' Vision: An Introduction to the Faith of John and Charles Wesley*. Downers Grove, IL: Intervarsity, 2004.

deSilva, David A. *Praying with John Wesley*. Nashville: Discipleship Resources, 2001.

Gooch, John O. *John Wesley for the 21st Century*. Nashville: Discipleship Resources, 2006.

Job, Reuben P. *A Wesleyan Spiritual Reader*. Nashville: Abingdon, 1997.

_____. *Three Simple Rules: A Wesleyan Way of Living*. Nashville: Abingdon, 2007.

Knight, Henry H. III. *Eight Life-Enriching Practices of United Methodists*. Nashville: Abingdon, 2001.

Strong, Douglas M., et al. *Reclaiming Our Wesleyan Tradition: John Wesley's Sermons for Today*. Nashville: Discipleship Resources, 2007.

Yrigoyen, Charles Jr. *Praising the God of Grace: The Theology of Charles Wesley's Hymns*. Nashville: Abingdon, 2005.

ABOUT THE CONTRIBUTORS

Michael J. Coyner is the resident Bishop of the Indiana Area of the United Methodist Church, and he has served as President of the Board of Discipleship for the 2005-2008 quadrennium. He has earned degrees from Purdue University (B.A.), Duke Divinity School (M. Div.), and Drew Theological School (D. Min.), along with honorary doctoral degrees from Dakota Wesleyan University and Evansville (Indiana) University. After serving as a clergy member of the North Indiana Conference, he was elected a bishop in 1996 and assigned for two terms to the Dakotas Area (1996-2004), before being assigned to the Indiana Area. He is the author of several articles and three books published by Abingdon: *Making a Good Move* (1999), *Prairie Wisdom* (2000), and *The Race to Reach Out* (2004).

Henry H. Knight III is Donald and Pearl Wright Professor of Wesleyan Studies at Saint Paul School of Theology, Kansas City, Missouri. He received his Ph.D. from Emory University in Theological Studies. He is author of *The Presence of God in the Christian Life: John Wesley and the Means of Grace, A Future for Truth: Evangelical Theology in a Postmodern World, Eight Life-Enriching Practices of United Methodists*; co-author with Don E. Saliers of *The Conversation Matters: Why United Methodists Should Talk with One Another*; and co-author with F. Douglas Powe of *Transforming Evangelism: The Wesleyan Way of Sharing Faith.*

Sarah Heaner Lancaster is Professor of Theology at Methodist Theological School in Ohio. She received her B.A. degree at Rice University, her M.Div. at Perkins School of Theology, and her Ph.D. in the Graduate Program of Religious Studies at Southern Methodist University. She is a clergy member of the North Texas Conference. She is the author of *Women and the Authority of Scripture: A Narrative Approach*, and she has written several articles in Wesleyan Studies.

Randy L. Maddox is Professor of Theology and Wesleyan Studies and Associate Dean for Faculty Development at the Divinity School, Duke University. He holds the B.A. degree from Northwest Nazarene College, M.Div. from Nazarene Theological

Seminary, a Ph.D. in theological studies from Emory University, and is an ordained elder in the Dakotas Conference of the United Methodist Church. Maddox is the author of *Responsible Grace: John Wesley's Practical Theology*, a contributor to *Wesley and the Quadrilateral*, and editor of *Aldersgate Reconsidered* and *Rethinking Wesley's Theology for Contemporary Methodism*.

F. Douglas Powe Jr. is Associate Professor of Evangelism, holding the E. Stanley Jones Chair, at Saint Paul School of Theology, Kansas City, Missouri. His Ph.D. is from Emory University. He is a local pastor in the Heartland Central District of the Missouri Conference. He is the co-author (with Henry H. Knight III) of *Transforming Evangelism: A Wesleyan Way of Sharing Faith* (2006); and a contributor to *God Delivers Me: A Model for Strengthening the Black Church in the 21st Century* (2008 forthcoming).

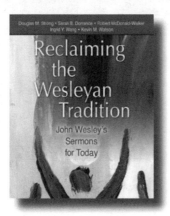